Master Or Myth
"Avoiding Bruce Lee Imposters"

By Peter. Canavarro

Copyrights© By Peter. Canavarro

ALL RIGHTS RESERVED.

No part of this book may be reproduced or transmitted in any form by any means, electronic or mechanical, including photocopying and recording, or by any information storage and retrieval system, except as may be expressly permitted in writing from the author.

Introduction

Granted my present level of experience, the opinions exposed in this book are very unlikely to change. However, I remain open minded to the possibility of being corrected by someone wiser, who may perhaps be able to see things differently.

Because, so many people claim to be Masters and yet, knowing enough to recognize one, seems to make them a rare find, I started this book intending to dethrone those whom in today's Martial Art world may reign through deceit.

However, in retrospect of how presumptuous such an aspiration can be, my hope is now that it may simply give someone the advantage of having an insider's perspective, before entering the Martial Arts quest.

This book is for all those looking for guidance in finding their true Martial Arts Master and avoiding imposters.

TABLE OF CONTENT

The Birth of a Myth 1

The Uncanny Master 5

Amazing Breaking Techniques 21

The Belt Ranking System 45

The Endless Road 49

Martial Arts, Inc. 52

The Black Belt 58

Defeating the Martial Artist 72

Upholding Tradition 74

The Sprouting Seed 92

The Mental Nutrient 94

Although most of the stories here related are based on true events, some have been changed to better represent the author's point of view.

Written and illustrated by

Peter R. Canavarro

THE BIRTH OF A MYTH

Modern day martial artists have not been the first ones to recourse to less than ethical practices, in order to enhance the illusion of super-human powers.

As far back as feudal times in Japan, old tales of fantastic feats were also mostly born through such practices.

One such famous tale started during a festive occasion when the warlords got into an enthusiastic debate over whose warriors were the best.

In order to leave no doubts, the hosting warlord finally proposed that the best warrior should settle the argument once and for all, by bare handedly killing a particularly ferocious bull, that was among the traditional gifts presented by his noble guests.

Much to the warriors' dismay, they were left with no choice but to risk their lives, by either refusing to honor their warlord's challenge (an act punishable by decapitation) or again facing death by enduring confrontation with a nine-hundred-pound bull.

At one warrior's request, the event was scheduled for one week later, in order to allow (as he put it) "time to prepare himself and sharpen his skills".

The days of rigorous training that followed seemed too little time for the warriors to farewell their families, in anticipation of the upcoming event quite possibly becoming a one-way trip.

In a small arena, surrounded by many villagers and warriors of the region, the impressive prize bull, infuriated by all the activity, had already killed or seriously injured several warriors, who had foolishly ventured into the arena.

When our friend who had requested the week of training was ordered to proceed, a silence of sympathetic fear set in among the crowd.

As the warrior entered the arena, dressed in a bright red silk kimono, the bull was still unaware of his presence and kept on ferociously sharpening its horns against the surrounding wood fence.

Reaching closer to the bull, the warrior suddenly assumed a bizarre fighting stance, and with all the intensity that his body could sum, he produced his loudest "Kiai[1]".

The warlord himself could not believe his own eyes. The bull turned, ready to charge, but at the sight of the warrior, it cowardly stepped back with a blood-curdling sound, as if crying in terrible fear.

From that day on, the storytellers spread the word about this Master whom the Earth itself feared, for the ground shook at the sound of his "Kiai" and the wild beasts fled in fear of his cold stare.

---

[1] A shouting like sound.

Large numbers of Martial Artists came from far regions, hoping to learn his secrets and so the castle prospered and the warlord got richer.

The truth is that the only power that this one warrior had over the other challengers was the power of conniving intelligence.

Every night, during the week leading to the event, while everybody was sleeping, the warrior had visited the stables and very methodically, followed a little routine.

He would start by calling the bull's attention with his loud Kiai and waving his kimono inside the fence.

As the bull would, instinctively, start to charge against the red silk, he would mercilessly thrust a thin long needle straight up the poor animal's nostrils.

Anyone who knows about bulls will tell you that they are not very smart animals, but there just isn't enough stupidity even in a bull, to suffer such terrible pain and not learn sooner or later that a Kiai from a man dressed in red silk meant a needle up the nose.

And so, another "Grand Master was born...!

The Uncanny Master

Where does he come from?

How is he qualified?

Let us suppose that, after growing up in the U.S., you would decide to move to another country, ending up in some foreign city, where people never heard of football.

Once there, you decide to open a club to coach football and find out that the local authorities do not require special proof of your credentials, nor for that matter, do they demand any special qualification process. All you need is a business license, that can be obtained by simply paying a few dollars.

You then remember how one time you had been lucky enough to be a "towel-boy" during one of the national team games and how, in high school, your friends that ran the school newspaper, once voted you best quarterback. So, with the help of one of your first students, who just happens to be in the advertising business, you finally present your brochure.

Your picture, in a sweated football uniform, looks really impressive, especially since the Super Bowl crowd, in the background, seems to be cheering for you.

Some years later, as your success grows, you may have actually become respected as one of the most recognized experts in that country. Who would then dispute the credentials proclaimed by your brochure?

"Title holder for the best quarterback in 1974. After retirement from playing, assisted the Giants to victory in 1990."

Comparatively, this should give you the answer to the questions pondered at the beginning of this chapter! As farfetched as it may appear a few years ago, this is how a great number of the so-called Martial Art experts came to exist in America. Particularly, after the Bruce Lee movies made the popularity of Martial Arts surge fantastically World-wide.

Just like the hypothetical situation described above, they were merely able to coach the basics of a particular Martial Art style that was familiar to them.

In this case, however, things got more complicated because the official Martial Arts organizations of their countries, realizing the potential of what was taking place, started sponsoring their own representatives.

These ambitious individuals could rank as low as second degree black belts, who, once promoted to honorary, (alias fictitious), sixth and seventh degrees, left their homeland in search of the American Dream.

With its members tied to the responsibility of paying back royalties, while popularizing their style, these organizations controlled and profited well from the exploits of the Western public. But as the money involved grew bigger, their protegees got wiser and started to form their own independent Federations, ending the relationship.

Their success resulted from being able "to see in a blind man's land", more so than from their talents as teachers or their qualities as great Masters.

Back home, they would have been lost among thousands of others, equally mediocre.

The credentials, written in most brochures, accompanying some dramatic pictures such as a stack of bricks being pulverized by an amazing hand blow, are usually as dubious as the integrity of just such bricks.

They claim to be Sixth Degree Black Belts, winners of some obscure national title, that may sound very good but really means very little.

Master Funachoshy, one of the forefathers of the Martial Arts, after a long life dedicated to karate, claimed to only be a humble Fourth Degree Black Belt.

Rank has become a commercial race, and some instructors will spontaneously pronounce themselves as high as Tenth Degree because that's what attracts the public.

Very few people in the United States legitimately hold ranks over Fourth Degree, and from those, fewer yet could truthfully live up to a Master status.

I must interject that by saying legitimate, I am referring to the true sense of the word and not some sort of "official" recognition.

Titles and diplomas are found "a dime a dozen" in the Martial Arts which not only undermines most official legitimacy in this field but also does not very often preclude the honored party from being incompetent.

On the other hand, the absence of such "official" recognition does not necessarily exclude the existence of supremacy in those who may have chosen to alienate themselves from the ego battles and politics so characteristic of such entities.

A Black Belt of any degree, a strong body with excellent technique, and good fighting ability are all qualities of a great warrior, but to a Master, they are only parts of a greater whole.

Despite this, it is very common to find individuals who apparently believe that a constant demand for respect from others, simply added to the qualities listed above, automatically makes them worthy of the title of Master.

As a matter of fact, this leaves an immense void to be filled. The word "Master", defined as one eminently skilled in any pursuit, has a certain connotation in the Martial Arts, that surpasses this basic definition.

Like in most Arts, a Master is someone who transcends the conceptual parameters of technical execution, evolving into his own style, through an insightful development of personal characteristics.

The distinction between the Master and a Grand-Master is just a pretense to vulgarize the former.

These titles should not be used gratuitously so that such honor can be reserved only for those who actually are grand.

Mastery in Martial Arts does not imply anything different than in any other form of Art.

A very talented sculptor, just out of college, regardless of his ability, would never think of proclaiming himself a Master of his Art.

Even after years of developing and establishing his own style and gaining recognition from his peers and disciples, he would still be taking a chance at being scorned, or deemed pretentious, if he upheld himself equal or superior to Michelangelo.

I guess the difference is that in this case, the person laughing is less likely to receive a beating and also, therefore, less likely to be intimidated into submissive respect.

The general public's stereotype of a Master in Martial Arts is usually embodied by an older Asian man of exemplary behavior and humbleness, whose eloquent teachings, full of grace and wisdom, are backed up by the power of the Art that he has mastered over the years.

In fact, one may note that these days the only questionable variables would be that he does not necessarily have to be of Asian race or old. (Although, to find a very young man with these qualities, would be uncommon.)

If it were possible. To make all the so-called "Masters" live up to this stereotype and compare Martial Arts with painting or music, we would have a world full of "DaVincis and Beethovens".

Unfortunately, what one so often encounters is an abundance of painters by the hour and back-alley troubadours.

*

"I have over twenty years of experience in the Martial Arts."

*

This so often heard statement, part of the common business advertising, has in most cases, a similarity to pouring water into a glass…; Eventually, not stopping will result in spilling, rather than adding to the content.

If someone told you that he had over twenty years of experience in driving, would you, therefore, assume that he was an expert race car driver, or for that matter, could you even conclude that he was actually a good driver?

Surely logic would demand any believable conclusions to come only after actually witnessing a display of his abilities, or, undoubtedly, after discovering that he actually had raced in the Indianapolis 500.

I don't believe anyone took Dustin Hoffman seriously, when he, playing the "Rain Man" character, kept emphatically proclaiming to be an excellent driver.

In a similar parallel, for the Martial Artist's experience to have any relevance, there must be some essence to the time spent during all those claimed years; Something that will transcend the average dedication of three hours per week, during the initial four or five years (in order to get a 2nd degree Black Belt), and a subsequent 16 years of running the business affairs of a Martial Art school.

Still today, the mystique surrounding the Black Belt appears to prevent people from having the most simple common sense doubts, as they would probably have in a similar situation when inquiring about any other form of Art, which they may not be familiar with.

It makes one wonder. If the "Rain Man" wore a Black Belt around his waist and proclaimed to be an "excellent Master", would there be someone willing to give him the benefit of the doubt.

The very act of perceiving oneself as a Master contradicts the principle that he should be regarded as such only by others, despite the noble intention of humbly concealing his strength.

It is not always easy for a novice to be able to look past the smoke screens and search for the qualities that can actually make a difference; those that may start at the most basic level with something like a teacher's ability to properly communicate.

For this, one must possess more than just basic knowledge of the language. He must actually be able to speak like a teacher.

Let us face it, and philosophical and profound message is going to lose a great deal of its strength, without effective prose, a little sagacity, and some wisdom.

Before even discussing the value of the content itself, perhaps I am being overly critical, but when lecturing starts something like this:

--- *"You's have to understand that we's..."*

I think that it is off to a bad start!

Possibly worse, yet, is the total abandonment of spirit fortifying teachings.

Many times they are misconstrued as religious or nonsense values by jock type teachers or are altogether avoided due to the difficulty that many foreign instructors have, to properly articulate philosophical concepts in English. (This assumes that in the first place, such knowledge and ability were ever present in their native idioms.)

Not even realizing the loss at hand, people seem to at times, simply become enchanted by the broken English normally derived from Asian phonetic influence, a characteristic that almost sets the standard for the way a Martial Art instructor should sound.

In order to claim a little more latitude in this criticism, without being accused of racism, (the furthest thing from my mind), I will start by offering my own embarrassing example.

I had just come to the US, and in an effort to make my high school English stretch to the slang used by all the other guys, I had come to realize that the word "chick" was at times used when referring to a girl.

Doubting that such an abbreviation would be a good addition to making my heavy accent understood, I decided to fully articulate the word as I said to my friends:

"I heard that many good looking "chickens" go to that club."

My friends almost "died laughing".

With that in mind, comes the recount of my novice struggle to understand one of my instructors, while he attempted to explain to our class the fine aspects of meditation.

Like all the others, I also felt that not much beyond breath in and breath out was decipherable from his heavy Korean accent, but the worst part was maintaining a straight face after his usual command ordering us to sit for meditation.

--"Evely (every) body Shit (sit) down."

In this case, if there ever was a profound thought able to get through that language barrier, it was lost in our struggle to, not burst out laughing at the comical beginning.

Finally, and more importantly, is the content of the message itself.

If one could attain just a small amount of knowledge, from every useless, boring speech, imposed by so many uneducated Martial Art instructors across the country, one would surely become a "walking encyclopedia".

*

A lecture to an adult class that can be comprised of an

amazingly diversified group of individuals, should not become a self-indulgent act or useless digression, provoked by an attack of mental diarrhea.

*

Beyond a certain amount of tack, some formal education in psychology is almost indispensable, unless one happens to possess an unusual ability to motivate and lead.

If in doubt of this need, one should ponder why this is a requirement for any other teaching certification.

On a more superficial analysis, one may try to disregard such evident inadequacies as secondary, but at times, the consequences can become worse than a simple knowledge imbalance.

Imagine yourself in a dangerous street confrontation, feeling very confident because of a gun that someone just gave you, after teaching you how to use it.

Now imagine your surprise, when you try to shoot and the bullets are blanks.

The surprise will quickly turn to shock, given the possibility that then, your opponent may be aiming the real thing in your direction.

The point is that, at times, misguided by poor instruction, people develop such a false sense of security, that, at best, it will eventually end up getting them humiliated, in some street tug, or worse, seriously injured, (possibly dead).

In other cases, the lack of physical education knowledge is so extreme, that some students develop chronic injuries, due to improper training.

One of the most common examples of just such negligence usually happens during rand promotion tests, when instructors will call upon the students to demonstrate their techniques, by way of breaking boards with bare hands and feet.

In most cases, they have neglected some or all necessary measures to provide proper conditioning of the body parts in use. So, the students will attempt to break the targets, either as a result of peer pressure or out of pure foolishness.

The counter-productive result is that, even if the attempt is successful in destroying the target, the students rarely walk away without some kind of injury.

This can be especially damaging in the case of young children, when bone calcification, still in the early stages of development, makes them much more fragile and, therefore, susceptible to more serious injuries.

By this, I don't mean to suggest the exclusion of breaking boards, as part of karate training.

In fact, I believe it to be quite indispensable, as a way to test one's conditioning of the body weapons and the effectiveness of the various techniques.

However, the technique in use and the body weapon of choice must be carefully selected, according to each individual.

Conditioning must be a methodic and supervised part of training, especially when preparing for bare knuckle punches.

This becomes even more important, on attempts where the targets do not break and the shock waves will bounce back to the practitioner's bodies, forcing them to "double over" in pain.

Without the density and callosities attained in preparedness for impact, this is when many serious injuries can happen.

The truth is that when a target breaks, even if the hand or foot has been conditioned, most often injury rarely occurs; and when it does, it is normally just superficial skin damage.

It would probably be fair to say that the ultimate test of one's conditioning happens when the target proves resilient to a strike, and whether the weapon will remain unharmed and ready for the next attempt.

The only exclusions that common sense should dictate, are head strikes, for there really isn't a non-damaging way of properly conditioning the head.

Besides, should the need ever arise to use it against an opponent's nose, the headache will surely be less painful or damaging than what it could be, from striking boards or cement slabs.

When a strike fails to break a target, it should be only from poor technical execution or from lack of focus and concentration.

However appropriate physical conditioning should still prevent the student from getting hurt.

The US government will license training establishments, such as Aerobics, Body Building, and Martial Arts, without requiring any sort of certification.

In some European countries, those individuals applying for such licensing must have a college degree in Physical Education and must provide the establishment with an attending certified MD, whose job is to examine and approve, or reject, every member, according to their health.

Of course, this does not mean that one cannot find good instruction in Martial Arts in this country.

Particularly, among some of the more traditional styles types such as Aikido, Judo, and Kempo, it seems to be relatively easy to find legitimate, well-structured instruction.

While failing to break a target, if a student "doubles over" in pain from lack of adequate conditioning, then bad instruction will have reduced a display of effectiveness into one of foolish self-destruction.

Master or Myth

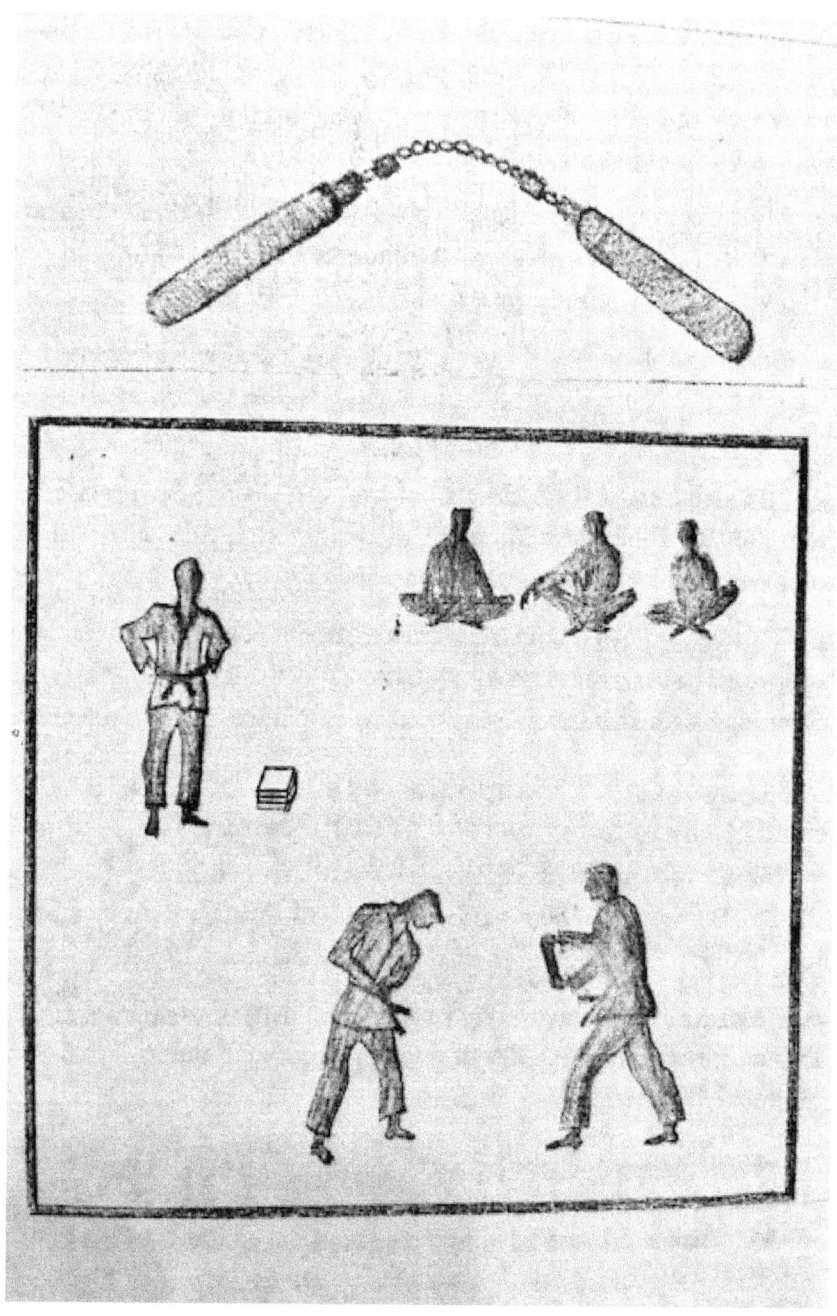

Even in more commercialized styles, such as Taekwondo, Karate, Kung-Fu, and Ninjitsu, one can find good instruction, although in these cases, the odds of walking into the right school, on the first try, are overwhelmingly unfavorable.

Most beginners will usually go to a school two or three times per week. If that is your case, when deciding on a school, you should first try to watch those classes for a while.

Besides talking to the instructor, ask some of the students (beginner to advanced), preferably outside of the school, if what you are searching for can be found there.

If walking in, while a class is in progress, do not be surprised or disappointed, if the instructor appears to ignore your presence and will not come to talk to you, until the class is over.

This is a sign of a conscientious teacher, whom nevertheless, will not one day stop teaching you, to attend to business. Besides, such action may already be an evaluation of your patience and character.

On the other hand, be cautious if one immediately stops teaching a class and attempts to sell you a three-year contract.

In far too many cases, schools have opened as branches, by individuals whose teachers have rushed them through the ranks, with the sole intent of widening their financial network.

The most unfortunate thing is that ironically, these places are far more successful than smaller, less commercialized, pure Martial Arts training halls.

Because they are usually in good comfortable locations, equipped with all sorts of apparatus, intended to make training more fun, they can even, for the most part, actually provide a stimulating physical workout.

So, if you are asking yourself what's wrong with that, the answer is nothing, as long as you realize that this is closer to being Aerobics than it is to being a Martial Art.

There is a certain paradox, in judging a teacher's abilities strictly by how good his student's physical skills are. Keep in mind that the main factor in the making of an excellent student comes primarily from the student himself, not the teacher.

Imagine a well-established famous Master with an overweight student, of middle age, with no athletic ability.

At the same time, take a novice Red Belt and give him a student, a fit young adult with natural athletic ability.

After three years the first student will not be excellent, but he will be a better fit and doing things he never thought possible. He will have turned into a better man, stronger, more confident, and enthusiastic about his training.

With a lesser teacher, he would have never made it past the first three months of training, and would probably remain wastefully more discouraged than he already was in the beginning.

The second student's physical skills may at one point have looked good, but if he didn't yet drop out, bored in his unchallenged great potential, consider how a more knowledgeable and experienced teacher could by then have molded and inspired him into excellence.

Such is in fact the case, with the best Martial Artists, who may have attended a not so good school throughout their beginning days, before outgrowing the teacher.

Most schools located in rural areas often seem to have a more physically able, adolescent group of students than those in more populated areas.

Not having to compete with other schools in the area, or even other activities that a city may offer, an incompetent teacher may easily find himself with a captive student audience and falsely suggest to a layman, to be a better teacher than in reality.

On the other hand, if the same layman walks into a school where by force of circumstances an excellent teacher may have to deal with a less capable group of students, he might tend to disregard the fact, that it took superior teaching skills, to bring those same students to their present level of physical skill.

All things considered, if faced with these choices one is best served by first reading a few books and finally choosing a school based on what the teacher can offer him, rather than others.

AMAZING BREAKING TECHNIQUES

In 1974 I saw, for the first time, a Taekwondo demonstration. I was then living in Portugal and that style was just being introduced in that country.

As part of a national promotion, General Choi, the president of the International Taekwondo Federation, had come to test my instructor, to sixth degree, along with another instructor visiting from Spain.

At that time, I was sixteen years old and had a blue belt in Judo, plus the equivalent of a yellow belt in Shotokan karate, and had just started Taekwondo.

Very foolishly, I considered myself quite an expert, especially since I had seen every Bruce Lee movie several times over, and, like most kids back then, I too had become an overnight "expert" in nunchucks (Fighting sticks linked by a chain. See top of figure on page 17).

That demonstration really impressed me and put me in my place, making me realize how little I really knew.

It was amazing when my instructor, executing a "jumping side-kick" broke five boards in a single blow. All this after leaping over eight students that formed a long human barrier, kneeling on the floor, side by side, in a squatting position.

Certainly, unbelievable was the height of some jumping around and front kicks, such that the holders actually had to stand on top of chairs while holding the boards.

However, in retrospect, it is now quite disappointing to realize that the short student standing on top of the chair holding the boards at mid-chest level, had them only slightly higher than if a person of average height, standing on the floor, held them leveled above his head.

But in all fairness, since the boards still remained at a height that not everybody could kick, this was an almost forgivable way of making it look more impressive.

Unfortunately, the more one learns about Martial Arts, the more evident it becomes how so many people resort to deceit.

I should probably be thankful for an event that, quite possibly, redirected me from following in the footsteps of those I today criticize, but despite the many years that passed, embarrassment still remains as the most vivid recollection of that moment.

With my black belt promotion test forthcoming, I had started to condition the fingers of my right hand in order to attempt a Spear Finger[2] * break through one board.

Two months before the test I started the mornings and ended the days doing "push-ups" on my fingertips.

As my instructor suggested, I filled a bag with beach sand and spent at least one hour a day trying to penetrate each strike of my Spear Finger technique, deeper and deeper into the sand.

After the first three or four days I had to stop, for the pain caused by the skin separation under the finger nails made it intolerable to continue.

A few days passed by, but as soon as I anxiously started again, the bleeding immediately reoccurred and the pain became worse than ever.

---

[2] See Page 27

It was then that my wife suggested the use of dish-washing gloves, as she rationalized that it would still give me the strength training, without the damage of abrasion.

Within a couple of weeks, I was able to confidently strike the sand with full power, penetrating it with my hand deep enough to cover the whole wrist.

By progressively adding water to the sand this became harder, but I could feel my fingers getting stronger almost day by day.

The last two weeks of December, as it became traditional, we closed the school for Christmas and my wife and I flew from Florida to visit our family in Pennsylvania.

I remember my mother affectionately calling me crazy, as the evening would come and I would passionately keep pounding into my trusty sandbag, while everyone else would sit around watching television.

When the day of the test arrived, in the midst of January, I still felt quite nervous. Despite all the training, those boards were a lot harder than the wet sand...!

As the moment of truth arrived, I was walking towards the pile of boards to select the would-be target, when, unexpectedly, my instructor called me to the judges' table at which he presided.

After requesting to see my hand, and carefully observing it from both sides, he and one of the guest Masters who sat beside him exchanged some quick words in their native Korean language, leaving me perplexed and wondering what was going on.

Unprecedentedly, my instructor got up from his chair and, searching through the wood pile, selected one board, which he handed to me, telling me to proceed.

As I was looking at the board and saw that it was obviously cracked, I could feel a hot flash rushing through my body, making my face inadvertently blush.

In confused dismay, my eyes quickly lifted from the board, searching him for an explanation, but at his patronizing reaffirmation that I should proceed, I could not help from thinking that in his experience, by looking at my hand, he must have realized that I was not ready for a real board, and he was, most likely, just trying to prevent me from getting hurt.

His devastating assertiveness in the way he told me to use that board had wiped away my self-confidence.

As I walked to the center of the floor, fighting my self-doubt, I placed the board (cracked-side down) bridging the top of the two concrete blocks used as supports.

It was then it happened…!

Humiliation and embarrassment set in, as one of the assistant black belts who helped me set up the break, very discretely inspected the board, surely in disbelief, for my endowment to perform such a difficult technique.

As I helplessly watched him lift the board and realize that it was cracked, everything appeared to be happening, like a movie played in slow motion.

I felt a burning sensation in my gut, and all surrounding noise seemed as if it was being muffled by the echo of his remark resonating inside my head:

"Aaah… Ok…! Aaah… OK! Aaah… OK!"

Even though this happened sometime in the middle of my test, I can't remember much of what happened after, except for the devastating, complacent smile on that assistant instructor's face.

Because I missed my forms, and probably much else of whatever I may subsequently have done, passing that test only served to make me further disillusioned.

A whole week passed by in which I stayed away from the school.

The simple thought of any subject relating to Martial Arts seemed to trigger the image of my "buddy's" face and his demeaning comment ("Aaah… OK!"), which was really as saying: Now I understand how you can do this.

I was very surprised when at work the doorbell rang one morning and I found my instructor standing there.

After taking a little tour of my office, we sat down and he tactfully brought the subject up, and I ended up telling him all about the way I felt.

Prematurely anticipating some sympathetic words, which would have been surely destined to fall short of satisfactory, I was sort of surprised when already holding the keys to his car, he stood up and merely said:

"I understand…! I will see you at the school tonight. Come early: one hour before class time."

When I walked into the school he was sitting in his usual spot, by the window, reading the newspaper.

In the middle of the floor, I could see the two cement blocks, with a board already positioned and awaiting me.

After changing into my uniform, I came out of the dressing room to find him already standing by the board.

"I am sorry, I did not realize that you were ready for this, but after our talk today, I know that it was my mistake!."

With these words, he stepped back and simply pointed to the board, suggesting that I would execute the break.

We both laughed as I picked the board up, making sure that it was not cracked.

When I hit that board, for all I cared my fingers could even have broken, for I was not about to hold back that time.

Fortunately, without any problem, they speared through the board, breaking it in half.

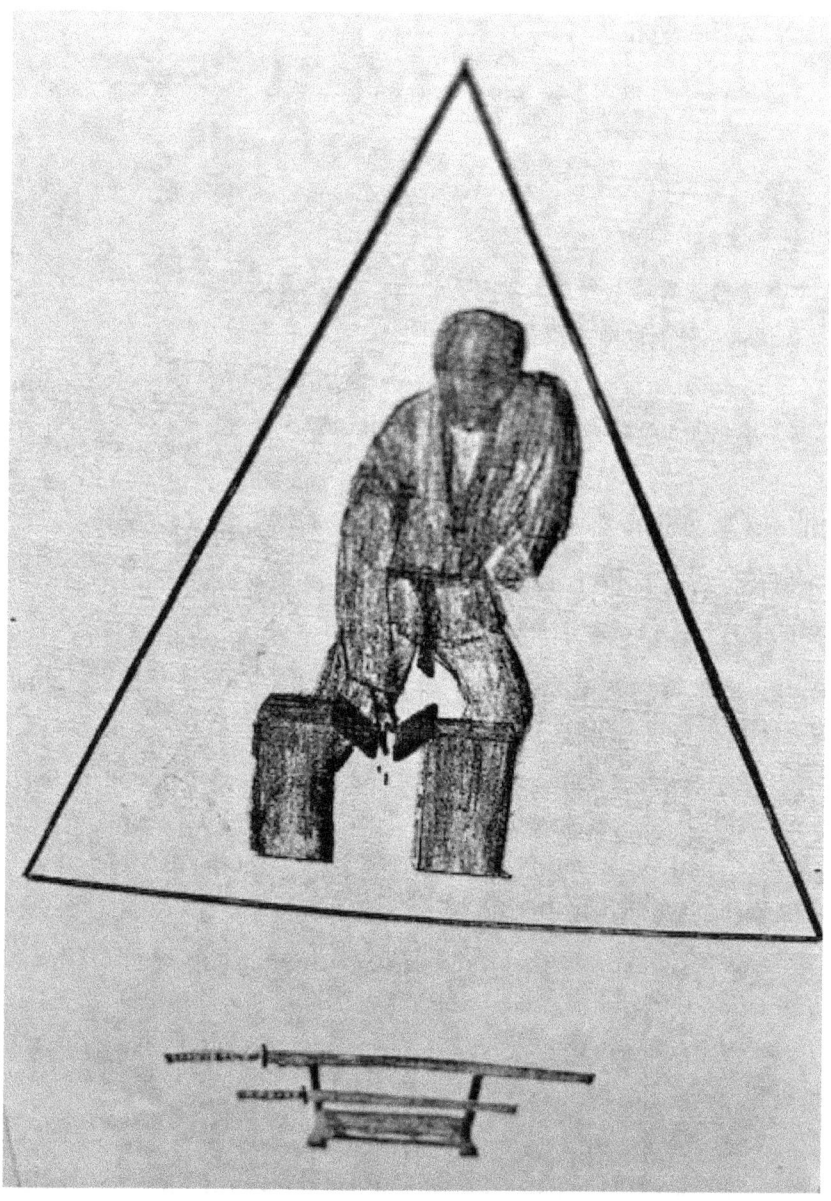

However, as quickly as it came, the satisfaction of that moment was gone, for, as I told my instructor, this still could not redeem me in the eyes of the one that troubled my conscience.

"*So,*" he replied:

"*Only three people knew that the board was cracked; you, me, and the other instructor.*

"*We both know now that this is irrelevant since the ability to perform this technique was already within you.*

"*So, next time you see his mistaken smile, this knowledge should give you the strength to smile back and the comfort to find peace within yourself.*"

I always cherished that lesson and often told it to my students, yearning to deter them from making that kind of mistake.

I don't believe that my buddy ever came to know this, but there is still the possibility that one day he may get to read this book.

However, I did get my satisfaction from a similar situation with him, about five years later.

It happened in a Fort Lauderdale tournament, during the finals for the breaking competition.

Bridging two cement blocks were two boards on top of each other. Although they measured the usual ten inches square, everyone's attention had been captured by virtue of their unusual thickness (a solid two and a half inches each).

This had become sort of my trademark break, and as both hands simultaneously delivered a double bare-knuckle punch, breaking through the two solid boards, I obtained second place in that competition.

Even though an impressive side-kick through ten concrete slabs gave my buddy first place, I was still enjoying my little moment of glory when, in a déjà vu reply, he had inspected one of my boards after confirming its integrity, and had put it back.

After my performance I knew he was impressed when, walking by me, with tightened lips and affirmatively nodding his head, he simply murmured:

"Hum… I like that!"

If only he knew how those small words had managed to finally lift my guilt, which weighed in the back of my mind during all those years…

The days of such mistakes seem an eternity away, lost forever in naïve pretentiousness that may conceivably be forgivable. But there just can't be an excuse for individuals of high rank and experience to purposely set out to fool the layman.

One such, most pitiful, demonstration that I witnessed took place during a Miami Open Tournament.

At the time, I had a small Taekwondo school in Pompano Beach, so I had gone to see the demonstration, along with a few of my students.

It all started very well, with some lower ranking Black Belt instructors, who despite the less highlighted, but extremely difficult techniques, showed superb execution.

However, it wasn't until the "Grand Masters" started that the audience really got excited.

With a fantastic "Roundhouse" kick, one of them broke clean off the neck of a whiskey bottle, leaving the decapitated part still undisturbed.

When the standing ovation was over, one of my students who had noticed my refrain from applauding, turned to me and said:

"I guess you are not impressed, huh?"

His tone of voice left an undefinable borderline between a criticism of my reaction and a wondering question of my ability to equal such a fantastic feat.

Ordinarily, I would probably leave such a remark from a beginner student hanging on a smile, but in a blessing of momentary inspiration, my reply came, as if by reflex"

"To see someone short change a blind man is not really very impressive."

Even though the frowning of his eyebrow was telling me that I was making little or no sense to him, by then the demonstration was already captivating his attention, again saving me from further explanation.

I was rather happy with that lucky stroke of inspiration, for without knowing it, he had just given me the subject for my next class.

Before leaving, I discretely picked up the broken bottleneck, gave it to that same student, and asked him to bring it to our school for the next class.

I spent quite a long time staging my little farce, just to illustrate who was the blind man being "short-changed".

So, when the time came for the next class, I had already set up in the front of the room some of the more fantastic feats as seen in the demonstration.

That night, when the class came to my attention, I had been patiently waiting by the props, making sure that no one came near or touched them.

Since we were located in a small shopping center, word of a special event had, somehow, gotten around, and so we have gained a small audience from some of our neighboring merchants and curious shoppers.

Despite everyone's expectations, training had progressed as usual.

I was not about to show to all those people the secrets of the Masters, without them first seeing the good side of Martial Arts training.

Nor was I going to miss the chance to use the students' excitement to orbit their energy into a more vigorous, high spirited, training session.

We must have covered every aspect of training that night. From meditation and breathing exercises to maximum exertion calisthenics, from sparring and self-defense tactics to forms, all the way into a cooling stretching period, finalized by a philosophic and inspirational speech about honor.

I was pleasantly surprised to see that a little over half of our initial audience was still there when we got to the end, for I was almost sure that they would all have left by then.

In fact, we even gained from among them one new student who later came back that week to join us.

But finally, the long-anticipated moment had arrived, as I asked all the students to sit facing the props.

Without any explanation and walking to the first station, I started to dramatically mimic the same ridiculous gestures and theatrical breathing that we had seen in the Miami demonstration.

Everyone enjoyed a good laugh when suddenly I stopped to say that if one didn't do this, the break would not be successful.

More seriously this time, I delivered a carefully calculated "Round kick", directing the ball of my foot to the neck of the bottle, which was identical to the one used by one of the "Grand Masters".

Everyone's amazement was quickly defused with the explanation of how I sawed around the bottle top, so it would easily fall at the slightest impact.

When I asked everyone to compare the broken glass with the one brought from the demonstration, it became evident that it also had been cut.

Not only the glass was equally even, but it also had been cut at the baseline, making the two pieces exactly the same size.

Despite the fact that they were now suspicious, I still managed to falsely arouse quite a sensational stir when the blow of my hand shattered the massive stack of ice blocks from the next prop.

Naturally, I then explained how, during the previous days, one at a time, the blocks of ice had been broken and then re-frozen to appear intact.

The next prop was an apparently solid stack of six square pine boards (each 10" X 10" X 5/8"), tightly held together by filament tape.

Although my bare-knuckle punch broke the stack of wood being held by one of my assistants, by then I could no longer fool the audience. This time there was no clapping – just disappointed silence, as they heard me explain that all the middle boards had been carefully selected for having weakening cracks running through their centers, and one by one, had been placed between the two that were cracked only on the inner side.

Remembering the Miami demonstration and all the comments made that day on the way back home, clearly, the most talked about would be the subject of my next trick.

On top of a metal plate, there was a piece of hard white stone, kidney shaped and critically supported at both ends by two other alike stones.

When the "Grand Master" delivered his hand blow, everyone was amazed at how hard the stone seemed to fragment under the tremendous impact of his would-be omnipotent hand.

I particularly remembered, at the time, the naïve smile on the face of one of my students, as he rejoiced in admiration:

"Can you imagine, getting hit by that hand?"

As the same feat was now reproduced by my hand, the explanation was given, while facing him directly:

"It really wouldn't be any different to get hit by this hand!"

The truth is that the hand simply pushes the top stone down, forcing the round edges to slip off from the two base stones. The impact against the hard metal plate is what actually causes the stone to shatter into pieces.

Seizing the opportunity to add a little humor to the situation, I didn't even think how "corny" it must have sounded when, holding the metal plate above my head, I turned to the students and said:

"Now, can you imagine getting hit by this plate?"

A relaxed laughter filled the room, but it quickly shifted to a nervously unsettled murmuring as I requested a volunteer and unveiled the shiny blade of my Samurai sword.

As I had hoped, one of my senior students and long-time friend stepped forward. To this day I don't know for sure if he did it out of trust or if by the knowledge of what was about to happen, but, either way, there he lay on the floor, in bare torso, holding a watermelon across his stomach.

Let me just add that the watermelon, besides its ideal texture, shape, and size, is a purposely gruesome choice for this demonstration because, at times, those with a weaker stomach have been known to pass out from mistaking its redness as one's inner parts.

In a single strike, the blade found its way through the watermelon, dividing it into two pieces and leaving the student unharmed (much to everyone's relief).

One by one the students got to feel the blade which, unlike the sharpness of a real Samurai sword, was as dull as a butter knife.

In fact, in the US it is difficult to find a sharp-edged sword. They are mostly made with the same kind of edge found in stainless steel silverware, which cannot be sharpened.

Needless to say, without cutting the person under it, there is a world of difference between the skill necessary to split a melon with a dull blade and the incredible accuracy and control required to do the same with a real sword.

Master or Myth

When we did this in our school the "victim" was lying on the floor, but during the demonstration, the person holding the melon was lying on a bed of nails, which made it much more impressive.

It reminded me of the time when some children students accidentally stumbled upon my instructor's bed of nails, which was used in similar demonstrations.

The kids had found the bed, stored in the back of the gym and, one by one, were laying on it, without any concern or difficulty.

The reason for this is that there are so many nails forming the laying surface, that each supports only a very small fraction of one's total body weight. By distributing the pressure in such a way none of the nails does more than lightly mark the skin of any person laying on it.

To help finalize my little charade my assistant was already holding the last prop. At the end of the long bamboo staff, attached by a fishing line, dangled loosely suspended a broomstick which measured approximately three feet in length.

I had intentionally saved this for last because it had been one of the feats performed by the lower ranking instructors at the beginning of the demonstration and despite its technical difficulty, it had gone unnoticed.

In Miami, with tremendous accuracy, the man had delivered a sidekick that broke a similar stick in half.

I started by explaining that I had examined the stick that he had used and it appeared to show no traces of previous cutting, therefore confirming what I already suspected, judging by the perfect execution of the kick and the breaking sound, this had been a legitimate breaking demonstration.

At my challenge, the students tried to break the similar prop that I had prepared, but without success. They sent it, time after time, into an uncontrollable swing.

Given the failure of their attempts, it was only a matter of time before one of them called upon me to demonstrate the technique. But I had different plans for that stick, as I explained:

"My kick, by breaking this stick now, will not give you the knowledge you seek.

This prop will remain in our school for all of you to gauge the quality of your side kicks.

When broken, it will be replaced.

After you all succeed once, if you wish, I will be glad to also break one."

After ending the class that night, I was pleased to see some of the higher-ranking students stay behind, still trying to break the stick; but as I would later come to realize, that training session had offered some benefits to me as well.

I had resisted the self-glorifying temptation of breaking that prop and prevailed in the intention to do what was right as a teacher…providing the students with a challenging orientation that, surely, would develop their sidekick skills more effectively.

Even though I knew that I could perform that feat, leaving all those people doubting that I could, was one more small step in my own conquering of the Martial Arts spirit.

That was a million times more rewarding and sustaining than a passing feeling of pride, which may have resulted from someone's momentary admiration over the simple breaking of a stick.

As the days passed some of the students managed to sporadically break one of the many sticks, as they would be replaced from time to time. However, they really seemed unable to consistently reproduce that feat.

One afternoon, after everyone else was already gone, I found three of the senior students attempting that break again. Although they had once before succeeded, that day their attempts seemed more futile than ever.

I thought it to be an opportune moment to intervene. So, I listened to their over critical comments concerning the technical details which they believed to be the cause of their failure.

But, as they became angrier, the thought of destroying the target had eclipsed any due concentration and the broomstick would simply swing further out of control, with each increasingly frustrated kick.

They had reverted to the primal instinct of progressively using more strength, forgetting the concept that they were told so many times, about how the destruction of any target should be incidental. Something that simply arises as a consequence of such a target standing in the trajectory of a perfectly executed technique.

This, as opposed to the target, becomes the purpose that gives reason for a technique to be launched.

Speed, focus, and technical execution, through improved repetition, should happen instinctively, allowing one's mind to concentrate strictly on strategy.

In a genuine state of readiness, no energy is ever wasted, worrying about the degree of resistance that a target (or an opponent) may oppose.

So, neglecting strategy, the students failed to hit the targeted stick slightly above the center, to better neutralize the pendulum effect, using a tight "knife edge" of the foot, close to the heel, where it offers a denser weapon.

Instead of drawing strength from the "know how" certainty of having been able to do it once before (which should make them devastatingly resolute), the excuse that the stick may have been stronger than the previous ones had served only to weaken their confidence.

I did, later, explain all of this, and over time some of them did eventually become able to consistently execute that break. But first, it seemed the right moment to demonstrate all the theory and (with a bit of a guilty feeling), enjoy their admiration and disbelief over how my seemingly lazy sidekick snapped that piece of wood with apparent ease.

As patronizing as it may sound, I knew then that their maturing would soon grant them a similar understanding to the one attained through my own previous countless failed attempts. So, at the time I saw no need for further explanation.

Such an understanding would surely be destined to dissipate any feelings of wonder, that they may have had at the time of my demonstration, but also, as my own experience would dictate, it actually constitutes the only way of learning most Martial Arts concepts.

Such concepts usually render most theoretical explanations useless. Without "hands-on" experience, even the most proficient instruction to the most open-minded novice can't usually achieve much more than a vague idea, without any practical application.

A couple of years before that day, during a promotion test, a group of my students being tested for Red Belt, had, one by one, failed to execute one of the requirements.

Holding two standard size pine boards (10" X 10" X .5"), at mid-level height with one hand, the students were expected to deliver a bare- knuckle punch with the opposite hand and breakthrough both boards.

The Grand Master for the organization that we subscribed to at the time, unable to personally attend the test, had a young Fifth Dan ("*godan*") ranked Master to oversee things and check on our progress.

Time after time the guest Master demanded the use of the same boards, as I witnessed with some embarrassment my students' futile efforts.

Standing at an impressive six foot five inches and approximately two hundred and thirty pounds in weight, one of my best hopefuls surrendered after three attempts, where with ferocious strength he managed to only project the unbroken boards across the room.

I remember thinking at that particular moment, that those boards must have been unusually hard, and if in the beginning I felt tempted to save face by executing the break myself, I now feared the embarrassment of being called upon by the guest Master and failing in front of all my students.

Shaking his head in disapproval, the small but robust Korean Master ordered that the same two boards be brought to him and, without ever losing the little grin on his lips, he effortlessly broke the two boards with a seemingly slow punch.

The test was over shortly thereafter and he never offered any guidance as to how to become able to do that, leaving everyone impressed with his only words:

"You must train harder."

I must admit that I also was impressed, but not as much by his strength as by his skill.

While everyone had focused their attention on the boards in suspense over whether they would break or not, I remember thinking that if that small man was sure enough of himself to even attempt breaking those boards after such a strong man failed, then he surely had some trick up his sleeve!

Master or Myth

My father, a magician by hobby, once told me that to unveil the secret in a magic trick, one must pay attention to every move, rather than concentrating on the object about to disappear. And so I attentively followed and memorized every single action.

Later, after everyone was gone and while holding another two boards, I repeatedly rehearsed the same technique, tracing his every step, one by one.

Even though I had previously experienced that type of strike with some success, by repeating the Master's execution in detail, I could hardly believe how easily the two boards succumbed at my first try.

I had read and heard before about the theory relating to the so called "Heavy Hand" technique, but only now, after experiencing it, did I truly understand it.

The next day, after our customary training, I called aside the newly promoted red belt students, eager to provide them with insight into my new findings.

I had started by replaying several times in my own mind, every movement employed in the Master's execution of his technique until finally narrowing down to two important factors that were absent when the students failed in their attempts:

First, by shaking his dangling hand, and opening and closing it repeatedly, he had forced the blood to rush to it, adding weight and density.

After compressing his closed fist against the tabletop, as if making it more compact and dense, the whole time as he positioned the boards and himself, he never opened his fist again. I had noticed his knuckles turning white from the tightness with which he clenched his fist.

The feeling my hand had when my hand hit the boards was best described as the action of a massive demolition ball swinging relatively

Master or Myth

slowly, but powerfully breaking through the outside wall of a building...the perfect visualization (I thought) of the "Heavy Hand" technique.

Visualization can be used in many different applications of the "Heavy Hand" technique.

Secondly, the left hand which held the boards, rather than remaining stationary, had traveled to meet halfway against the opposing force of the punch, therefore doubling the power of impact.

It was the comparable difference between the force created by a car crash against a wall while traveling forty miles per hour and the much stronger impact of it colliding with another car also traveling at the same speed in the opposite direction. The easiest way to increase speed and power while making it look effortless.

After explaining all these rational factors, it was beyond me why none of the students, who again held some new boards, were able to break them.

Led by the frustration of not being able to instantaneously induce such practical knowledge as intended by that logical and detailed explanation, I was beginning to question my teaching ability, when a snotty remark was murmured about it being easier to talk about it rather than doing it. I found myself inevitably having to demonstrate my conjecture.

Such as in learning how to ride a bicycle, where it becomes so easy once one knows how, also that break proved to be easy, by my hand, just as it had been the previous day.

However, at the start, regardless of how good one's explanation may be, most people would not be able to simply jump on a bicycle and ride it on the first attempt.

This was to become more of a lesson for me than for them...for no matter how much I tried to explain it, that feeling was just one of those things about Martial Arts that can only be learned over time, through practice, and self-enlightenment.

I recall later one of the students telling me:

"Boy...you really got the hang of that Heavy Hand Technique. I just don't think my hand is strong enough to do it...!"

In due time he was to become the first one of that group to understand and master that concept.

The Belt Ranking System

Starting with the white belt some schools may have as many as sixteen differently colored belts, each representing a progression in level of skill and knowledge leading to the 1st degree Black Belt (1st Dan, about three years).

2nd and 3rd Dan are normally the ranks in which most students will branch out into their own schools (about three to five years from 1st Dan).

Although practical expertise usually peaks around 4th and 5th Dan (about fifteen years after the 1st Dan), honorary rankings may continue to climb as high as 8th Dan.

Even though politics may play a major role (at times more than they should) in the attainment of such high ranks, they are supposedly awarded for special services that significantly contribute to the popularization of a style.

When properly implemented, a ranking system can be very useful to both students and instructors, particularly during the period leading up to the first level Black Belt. It not only serves as a reward for the students' progress, but each different colored belt becomes a short-term goal that, once obtained, cam provide a positive feeling of accomplishment. Also, it can help a teacher to study the amount and type of information given to each student and scale it in a logical timetable.

Secondarily (I must emphasize secondarily), the usual fees that students are expected to pay for these tests can serve as an additional source of income.

The instructor actually concludes before the test that the student is ready to advance in rank. Explaining that the true value of these tests is to evaluate the self-confidence with which a student can perform under pressure could, in fact, be counter-productive. As in many other situations, for that reason, a student often meets with many classically enigmatic explanations.

*

Among the beginning students, Sato listened attentively to the explanation of how during the next few months his progress would be constantly monitored until being determined that he was ready to advance in rank. At that time, he would be allowed to test for the next color belt.

Driven by his inquisitive nature and somewhat opinionated character, this would not be his first time as lashing a sarcastic question towards one of the lesser-able instructors. His contempt was particularly accentuated when it came to this one instructor, fueled each time he got to spar with him.

The fact was that the stocky built instructor, at the first sign of being cornered by Sato's natural fighting ability and superior athletics, would disarm the situation by inopportunely ordering the fight to stop. As if acting out of benevolent mercy towards the novice, he would then try to disguise his inability through some kind of patronizing advice, such as how trying to kick as high as the head was leaving his base leg very vulnerable to a sweeping technique. This, is despite the fact that he could not sweep Sato even if his life depended on it.

Such advice may have been in fact appreciated if coming from someone who may have just made Sato fall flat on his back, but otherwise, it just made him lose respect for his senior.

Peculiar, that the most devastating instructors, after mercilessly "cleaning his clock", always seem to choose some sort of flattering comment rather than a criticism. It could be something as simple as telling him how his blocking was getting so much better or, perhaps, how his ever-improving ability was making it, each time, more difficult to beat him.

Only then, almost inadvertently, they would give their advice:

"By you have better balance and speed...just so you are not so vulnerable to a sweeping technique."

Once again, as the instructor had finished his lecture about the beginner students having to earn their right to test, he found himself confronted by Sato's wise crack:

"If you already know that we can pass, why should we still have to go through the test!?"

With opportune timing, the Master had just entered the room, as he heard Sato's question. By quickly assessing the situation he had realized what a feeling of confrontation such tones had invoked. Foreseeing the fury of indignation that was about to shape the instructor's answer as one less than wise, he decided to intervene by calling everyone's attention with his calm and stern voice:

"That is an excellent question!"

Sato's arm pits tingled in startled reaction. Caught in his insubordination, he now expected the worst. However, the Master simply proceeded to move slowly to the big window that overlooked the mountains where the morning sun had just begun to rise. With a serene open hand gesture that seemed to unveil the beautiful view, he said:

"You saw the Sun rise yesterday...yet does that stop you from wanting to admire its beauty today?"

*

Although ambiguous, such an answer is always sure to take the wind out of the sails of the beginner student, curbing his spirit into a more harmonious disposition. As for the instructor, amidst his admiration for the Master's disarming wisdom and self-control, he recognized his own inapt loss of temper.

This would become another small step broadening his own perspective of the vast horizon still separating him from Mastery.

THE ENDLESS ROAD

Everyone can benefit, physically and mentally, from adequate Martial Arts practice. This holds true, regardless of gender, age, weight, height, strength, and intellectual or athletic ability. Ultimately, even those individuals afflicted with severe handicaps such as blindness or partial paralysis, have been known to enjoy practicing the Martial Arts.

Because of all these differences, it becomes necessary to adopt variable standards according to each individual.

Other than affording to, financially, wanting to do it may very well be the only requirement necessary to start training in any Martial arts. After it is everyone's prerogative to continue enjoying the physical and mental improvements that will almost undoubtedly take place. However, this should constitute one's main purpose and compensation on a personal level, not a side effect to wanting to become a Black Belt or a Master.

Disregarding it as such would be like discarding the fruits of an apple tree, just because they may not be sized as agricultural award-winning samples.

Similarly, the first season of Martial Arts must be taught to appreciate the benefits which can be collected along the struggle for excellence, no matter how small these may appear when compared to those of others.

Who knows? Along the way one may even become proficient in self-defense, may become a Black Belt, or even a Master (or not).

In terms of practicality, the best a good student should hope for is to defeat those with less experience and prove worthy against those who have more.

However, extending the honor of a Master title to any Martial Artist, on the grounds that he may own a school or be a good fighter, is like entering into the NBA Hall of Fame a four-foot-tall individual who, given his stature, happens to be a relatively good basketball player. Let's face it: not every practitioner can be a Master, just like not all jet pilots can be "Top Guns."

When personal maximum potential has been reached and minimum standards of style are evidently never going to be attained, rank should stagnate accordingly. In these cases, the door should not be left open to progression beyond the first Dan, unless, if you like with children, an honorary system is used to establish a clear distinction.

Another problem yet happening all too often is when the business-minded or financially desperate instructor decides to promote students just to be able to collect the test fees. These fees can render anywhere from fifteen to three hundred dollars, depending on rank.

In either case, the unfortunate result will always be another incompetent black belt.

By nature, (at least initially), the greatest majority of practitioners is not really composed of individuals that one would consider to be "fighters", nor do they usually possess very strong physiques. Those are the reasons why they sought Martial Art training in the first place and they also may be the reasons why so many Black Belts can be defeated when confronted with someone who may be physically superior or simply gifted with natural fighting ability.

Great fighters or warriors are not made by desire alone; most of them were already born "tigers", whom the Martial Arts have turned into Dragons".

The more common mutation from "pussy cat" to "tiger" may sometimes be asking too much with some people, but when it happens, it is only after many years of diligent practice and study, in the high ranks of Black belt (between 3rd and 5th Dan). The "Dragon Spirit", however, will be attained only by a few and will remain, for most, a distant horizon on an endless road.

MARTIAL ARTS, INC.

With its ever-increasing popularity, Martial Arts have become a substantial business. From and economic perspective an overview of it ranges from private lessons in someone's basement to acting roles in major motion pictures. Samurai swords, all types of knives, uniforms, and gadgets (most of it low caliber fake junk) are part of an endless variety of paraphernalia, ready to capitalize Martial Arts fever.

Despite a typical repetitiveness, new books continue to feature the authors, page after page, in a self-glorifying array of pictures, performing the same basic actions already found in hundreds of similar books. In them, the usual action shots depict the author performing dramatic skills that very often are questionable in terms of practical self-defense.

The attackers, with exaggerated theatrics, simulate expressions of pain, which border on the ridiculous and are intentionally chosen for being twice the size of the staring author, which in a real situation, would be more likely to give him a real good fight as opposed to allowing him to, as suggested, neutralize the attack.

In such works, one has to wonder if the intent to be informative was ever a consideration, or, if beyond the less than noble financial interest, simply remains egotism. The odds are such that I would almost be willing to bet that a random pick in the Martial Arts section of any book store would most likely leave one holding just such a perfect substitute for toilet paper.

Considering world advances in telecommunication it is actually hard to believe that anyone can, still today, impress and fool an audience by claims of mythical powers and superhuman feats.

Every time an individual uses the words "deadly" or "fatal" to describe his Martial Art style or ability, I have (admittedly) come to fall into a bad habit: it immediately triggers in my mind the image of those elixir salesmen as seen in the old western movies. They travel from town to town in their wagons, full of that miraculous "cure all" drug that was actually plain old tinted water. By this, they too made a living out of selling a lot of wishful thinking.

Any technique, either from a hard or soft style, can be made deadly by simply directing it to a vital area of the human body. A Judo hip throw can be used to direct an opponent, head first, against a hard concrete floor, breaking his neck and possibly killing him in seconds. More agonizingly, a karate blow to the throat can force the trachea to collapse, killing an opponent through desperate suffocation. One does not need to be a Ninjitsu expert to gruesomely direct an ordinary sharp object (such as a pencil) nasally through the skull into the brain area to create an instant job for the undertaker.

The fact is that the existence of these and other such drastic skills does not provide the attainment of a deadly individual, and certainly does not give any one an invincible fighting superiority. All Martial Arts can be deadly in theory, but even if someone has within himself the resolution to take another human being's life, added to the not-so-easy ability of applying such skills, it still remains a question of whether an opponent will make allowable the necessary opportunity to use them.

Ultimately it is one's opponent that determines the outcome of the battle. A Martial Artist is only as good as his opponent allows him to be...deadly or dead. (Extremes aside, victorious or defeated would be a better choice of words.)

In today's Martial Arts context, the word "deadly" is merely a marketing term, a ridiculous and clumsy attempt at inducting self-mysticism. Another smoke screen is meant to inspire respect where it cannot be attained legitimately. It is designed to make any novice believe that the myths are precarious pedestals intended to raise above the norm those otherwise lost amidst it.

Fighting ability of the "superman" in question is equivalent to the use of a gun.

Imagine a marksman, trained and extremely proficient in the use of hand guns (not your "average Joe") having a duel with the World's most capable Martial Artist, where at the start, both fighters would be standing about 15 feet apart. For the sake of argument, we will assume that a small caliber gun with regular bullets would be used, even if any expert gun fighter would most likely opt for the sure kill of a Magnum loaded with hollow point projectiles.

To further speculate, let us look at the conceivable unlikelihood that the unarmed man, with amazing agility and a little luck, would manage to dodge some of the first shots. Consider yet the hypotheses of him offering some less vulnerable parts of his body to lodge the next bullets and rapidly take advantage of a possible split-second hesitation on the part of the gunman, managing somehow to finally reach his would-be discredited opponent.

Even then, I would still rather be the gunman, for I guarantee that the next close-range shot would forgo any chance that my opponent ever had of walking from such a mismatch with body and soul still united.

The real advantage in a gun scenario is the one that the word "deadly" tries to falsely imply when referring to any empty-handed fighter. A superiority that no Martial Art can ever guarantee to anyone. Such myths are like a magnet capable of attracting paper…the green kind of paper.

*

Just outside their school some of the young pupils had playfully engaged in an enthusiastic debate:

"I would be like the tiger" one said, *growling his choice of what he believed to be the strongest symbolic animal of the fighting arts.*

"I would be the cobra because even the tiger knows that the tiger knows that its claws would be no match for any lethal fangs and speed."

Sato had intentionally reserved his comment for last. He was sure that no one could top his choice. So, as his colleagues turned to him, striking challenging poses that jokingly resembled the animals of their choice, Sato stood back a couple of steps and assumed the most macabre stances that his imagination could summon: he simply appeared to blow air through his mouth at the perplexed "zoo…"

"I would be the dragon and by my breath of fire only ashes would remain of both of you."

In the middle of the racket that followed, laughing and carrying on, none of them had realized the presence of the Master who kneeled behind the garden shrubs tending his flowers. As he stood up revealing his presence, the startled young students quickly came to attention and bowed to the old man.

"We don't allow tigers, snakes, nor dragons in this garden…go now",

He said with joyous laughter, while jokingly raising his shovel.

The next day during the entire training session Sato couldn't help noticing the small drawing that the Master had pinned on the wall at the beginning of the class. In it, designed with great passion and talent, a Dragon stood magnificently overpowering the fragile stature of a small man.

Sato knew right away that this had something to do with the episode from the previous day and that it surely was leading to one of those so-appreciated ways that his beloved teacher sometimes used when relaying the more meaningful messages of his wisdom. He could hardly contain his anticipation when the Master, gathering everyone around the drawing, brought things into perspective to all the students by relating his colorful version of a certain garden fight between these animals.

After repeatedly advising them that the answer he sought was in that drawing, he finally resigned to the fact that everyone remained of the opinion that the Dragon, Sato's choice, was undoubtedly invincible.

"I must tell you that I am somewhat disappointed, for it seems that you have learned very little after all this time of training.

"You are chasing the illusion that a dragon, something that doesn't even exist, is the most powerful warrior.

"The dragon is so powerful that, if nothing else, logic should make you realize that it can only exist in one's imagination.

"So, if you are the tiger or the cobra, despite your fears, if you decide to face the dragon you will realize that under that mask there is simply another man, who may perhaps be even more scared than you.

"One should never allow for others to use such myths to cloud the mind, or he will find himself surrendering to all kinds of dragons in the world before any battles even take place and one's strength has a chance to be tested."

While pointing to his drawing he had already begun to leave the room when, in between little mocking, sneers, his final comment was pronounced:

"Besides, this little man happens to be Prince Charming and we all know what he did to the big Dragon!"

THE BLACK BELT

Quite often training would take place outside in the yard behind the school. It was on such a day that the Master was confronted by Sato, one of his more promising students:

"Master, how long will it take for me to become a Black Belt?"

After a few seconds of silence, the Master pointed to a small tree nearby and said:

"When you can jump over that tree you will become a Black Belt."

No sooner had the class been dismissed when Sato rushed to the tree that stood almost six feet tall and immediately tried to jump over it. Despite several attempts, and such to the Master's amusement, neither Sato nor any of the beginner students who had followed him were able to clear the tree without getting tangled in the top branches and falling. One by one the defeated students started sitting on the ground attending to the bruises and scratches caused by the thorny tree. It was then that Sato complained with indignant frustration:

That is impossible! No one can jump that high!"

Without a single word and taking only a few short steps, the Master leaped over the tree, as if defying gravity with apparently effortless ease. The students were completely taken in amazement; they wondered what kind of special powers the Master possessed.

"Can you believe that?" one of the students asked, doubting his own eyes. It was then that grasping the myth of the moment the Master said:

"This is an ancient secret technique, one which I teach only to very special students who prove to be worthy of my trust."

As the students respectfully stood up and bowed to the Master, he made them promise unquestioned obedience and blind dedication as a condition for being taught the secret technique. So agreed, he proceeded to point to another tree just like the first one, but that one stood only inches from the ground and ordered the students to try jumping over it.

Sato had to bite his tongue, for he knew that questioning the Master's orders would mean not learning the secret technique, yet he could not stop wondering how jumping over such a small tree could possibly make him learn anything.

After every single student cleared the tree the Master turned to them and said:

"This is your little tree. Starting tomorrow you will come out here every day after class and again jump over it."

Even though none of the students understood the purpose of such an act, in time coming outside and jumping over the little tree became just another part of the daily training – soon taken for granted.

Three years had passed when one day the Master brought all the senior students to attention for a special announcement. Two students, along with Sato, had earlier been ordered to be present and waited already in the background. They were the only remaining ones from their class who had prevailed in their training since that day in the back yard.

Once signaled, one of the senior instructors quickly ran into the Master's chambers, returning with three brand-new Black belts, strategically placed across his extended arms. Ceremoniously, another one of the senior instructors took the belts one at a time and, while folding them in half, placed them in line on the floor in front of the Master.

Master or Myth

As their names were called, Sato and his companions were ordered to stand at attention in front of each belt.

"Today is a very special day," The Master continued with rejoiced pride: you have at last proved yourselves worthy of wearing your black belts – congratulations"!

After the ceremony, just as Sato and his friends were getting ready to leave, the Master asked them:

Now that you have become Black Belts, I was wondering if any of you would care to help demonstrating something to the beginning students who wait outside.?

Proudly the students immediately agreed to help and promptly followed the Master to the back yard.

Sato could not believe his eyes. It was a pathetic scene, as the beginner students clumsily failed to jump over "his little tree". Something that he believed to be so easy to do.

As the Master entered the yard one of the beginning students, whose face had even been scratched during his attempts to clear the higher branches of the tree, said in frustration:

"No one can possibly jump that high!"

One slight gesture from the Master's head was all the command necessary for Sato and the other new Black Belts to jump over the almost six-foot high tree in a patronizing leap.

"The reason why you cannot jump over the tree

Is because you haven't yet learned my secret technique."

Sato's eyes crossed momentarily with the Master's as they both exchanged a little smile. The secret was now his to keep.

After the beginner class had been dismissed the Master walked back to his new young Black belts and placing a small seed in the hands of each student he said:

"You have come the full circle by understanding

what a Black Belt is not! Now you must not

make the mistake of undermining it by taking

for granted your ability to do what

the new students can't."

With these words the Master seemed to finish his lesson and was already starting to walk away when Sato asked:

"Master, what shall we do with these seeds?"

The situation was all too familiar. The predictability of the novices has through the years allowed for the wise teacher to carefully stage these lessons to the point that he appeared to know exactly where he would be standing by the time Sato's question came.

So, as he faced the area where several different size trees had already been planted, he turned to them and replied with everlasting patience:

More trees must be planted…others will come

wanting to know our secret technique."

*

In many respects attaining the rank of Black Belt is the equivalent of a high school diploma. Even though they are both major personal accomplishments, one is likely to fall short of impressing anyone who can read or write as such as the other will not impress anyone who knows anything about Martial Arts. In both cases they are the mere basic tools that enable an individual to learn higher knowledge and eventually specialize as an expert in his field.

Dedication (above all), physical and mental capacities will dictate how far each individual will go. Unfortunately, so will politics and social status...but such is life.

The Black Belt is a symbol that should ascertain a specific level of knowledge and ability about a Martial Art style. The individual to whom such honor is bestowed should have proven his worthiness, not by just reaching his best (which in some cases may not be enough), but by developing the level of efficiency proper to being a Black Belt.

Such predetermined standard is what easily allows one to point a bad Black Belt from a good Black Belt student, but what it should do is prevent the bad one from ever existing in the first place.

It should be made clear at the start that for some people to become a Black Belt it may take longer than usual, and sometimes, as unfair as mother nature has made it, it may never even be possible.

The mental and physical ambiguity of human beings should not be used as an excuse to lower standards. In fact, if any changes are made, it should be to raise difficulty, so that above average individuals can still be appropriately challenged.

*

Sato had just come to discover that after his test, which anyone would agree was the best performance of the night, the Master had denied his presentation to the next week.

At the apparent unfairness of seeing all other students being promoted, even ones whom Sato had no respect for given their lacking abilities, he proceeded to, very inappropriately, question the old Master's decision, full of indignation.

If it were not for the Master's quick dismissal Sato would have undoubtedly suffered a nasty blow from one of the senior instructors that had already moved towards him, ready to punish such irreverence. As if alerted back to his senses, Sato bowed apologetically to both is seniors. He now remained slightly worried, not knowing that it was benevolent wisdom, rather than intent to punish, that motivated the Master into ordering that he would follow him.

In his office, as they sat, he placed a golden arm scale on the desk and by opening a beautiful black lacquer box that was lined in red velvet, he revealed a series of tiny identical weights.

"First, we shall look at the performance

of the other students: For every good aspect

we will place one weight on the right plate

of this scale, and for every bad one, the same

on the left side.

"Their technique may have been less than good

but they tried so hard that some of them almost

passed-out. They were too weak... yet with great

difficulty the had gotten stronger since the

last time."

One by one the tiny weights were added, but in the end, they remained even on both sides, keeping the scale balanced. Starting all over again, the little weights were added, this time to evaluate Sato's performance.

"Compared to the others your technical execution was

very good, but considering your physical

advantages if you had put forward an

equivalent amount of effort to that of the others,

you could have reached excellence.

"During the test your strategies were very good and smart,

but you neglect the teachings of Martial Art Spirit by failing to demonstrate compassion for some of the opponents with

less ability."

Respectfully to all the pros and cons, weights were added, always bringing the scale to an equal balance, until finally, by placing one last weight, the Master made it tip towards the side of the bad aspects, and he said:

"When you find the reason that made this scale tip,

You will have found your own balance. We will then

remove this last weight and you will advance to the

next rank."

Master or Myth

During the next few days, the Master kept his close attention on Sato's every action. He was pleased to notice how the student had now become much more careful when sparring others with less ability. That night he decided that it was time to conclude the young man's lesson and so he had him ordered again into his private chambers.

While pouring some hot tea into Sato's cup, he invited him to sit at the small table and asked:

"So, tell me, have you found yet the reason
why that last weight was added?"

"No, I have not, sir. I am sorry."

"Well, in that case I must explain: You see, it was your
indignation, the lack of humbleness and respect
all together demonstrated by your reaction to being
told that your rank promotion had been denied."

"But, Master, with all due respect, my test and its result both took place prior to that regretful moment, so how could you have entered in your decision?"

"Your reasoning starts from the wrong premise, my son…
you see, your test had not yet ended. In fact, the
announcing of that decision was intentionally planned
as the most important part of your test. Your instructors
and I actually awaited your reaction to make our final decision.
"The truth is that I had been informed by your instructors
that, although your physical skills were improving rapidly,
you seemed to lag behind in some other aspects."

Faced with his teacher's wisdom and the amazing predictability of his own foolishness, Sato stood up, and after apologizing in humble shame, he asked for permission to be dismissed.

Denying his request, the Master asked that he would remove the belt around his waist and while replacing it with a brand-new Black Belt, replied:

"Sometimes the ability to correct our mistakes becomes

a question of simply recognizing them. Learn from this

lesson how to better honor the trust I hereby place upon you.

Now you may go."

Ordinarily Sato would have probably left the Master's office and passed by the other students with a superior and proud stroll, showing off his new color belt and causing resentment from everyone around him. This time, however, he walked almost as if trying to hide his promotion.

With all the students as witnesses, he approached his senior instructor and in the middle of the training area, as he removed his new belt, he humbly declared with a bowed head:

"I realize now that I am not yet worthy of this belt,

So, I ask you to please keep it until you feel

that I really deserve it."

The instructor who seemed to already be predisposed to always having to reprimand Sato, was so surprised with this unexpected gesture that is reply, for lack of actually having something to say, was just a disoriented reflex:

Put your belt back on right now. If the Master

Has awarded you this belt, who do you think you

are to question his decision?"

Putting his belt back on, Sato was already leaving the room when the senior instructor, recognizing the uncalled abruptness of his answer, slowly brought his hands together, initiating an admiring applause that was soon joined by all the other students.

As Sato turned around the happiness of the moment had overwhelmed his heart so strongly that he had to dry swallow his upset feelings.

It was a good thing that the Master, who had discretely observed the whole situation, remained standing far away by the door to his office. Otherwise, he may have noticed his glassy looking eyes, wetted by some embarrassing tears which Sato tried so hard to disguise with a smile.

*

If one's faculties fall short of the prerequisites to become a commercial airline pilot, there is no reason why one shouldn't or couldn't still enjoy learning how to fly an airplane. While zipping through the clouds and with growing confidence, imagination and fantasy would transform the little single engine airplane into a powerful jet fighter. The quiet low altitude suburban flight would become a covert, radar-evading spy mission.

There really is nothing wrong with this! We may even add that, while imagining all the battle maneuvers, one's flying skills may actually improve. The absurd would be, once back on the ground, to allow fantasy to still propel our would-be Red Barons into proclaiming themselves Top Gun Pilots.

In that same parallel it may seem inconceivable, but some individuals are in fact perpetual White Belts, grounded by their own limitations, even after the belt around their waist has been changed to a different color.

The inadequacy is that excessive emphasis placed on becoming a First Dan often gives an erroneous purpose to the student's training and dedication.

By shadowing the more important daily benefits, soon they are taken for granted and many instructors will corner themselves into the habit of advancing students' ranks to maintain their interest and, doing so, by simple merit of attendance.

In discussing this problem with one of the Masters, under who's tutelage I once was and whose opinion I highly respect, I was told:

"In the beginning it is not important how good

or bad a practitioner may be. Much more

important is to first captivate his interest,

even if to do that you must promote him

to the rank of Red Belt faster than you would

like to.

"At that time, he will have become less likely to

drop out and you will then get the chance to refine

his technique before advancing him in rank.

"As an instructor you will be doing people and your Art

a better service by having a big school with hundreds

of bad practitioners, among whom you may be able

to eventually select a few excellent Black Belts,

rather than a little school with only a few excellent

Black Belts."

Even though I must accept the logic of his point of view, I underline the importance of applying it only up to the rank of Red Belt. Past that point, only those that truly qualify should be promoted in order to prevent the devaluation of the Black Belt.

DEFEATING THE MARTIAL ARTIST

It is always amusing to hear people suggest the undermining of the fighting Art's efficiency through quotes such as:

"My Martial Art is Smith and Wesson…"

If one was to answer this, assuming the same frame of mind, he could contend that given that type of confrontation, a Master would then recourse to his own "special Martial Art" …a machine gun.

Equally far from relevant, is also the classic tale about the Martial Artist who, shortly after warning his opponent about his experience as a Black Belt, finds himself ridiculed by a good old boy's punch.

To attribute such importance of representation to any such Martial Artist, would be no less absurd than to criticize the musical excellence and virtuosity of Mozart's piano concertos, through the performance of any common musician.

In this case most people would be likely to criticize the player for his incompetence and probably even deem him foolish for his unreadiness and obvious misrepresentation. Anyone wanting to witness Mozart's work come to life would surely look for a virtuoso musician, skilled with great ability.

By the same token, any individual chosen and capable of truly embodying a Martial Art would almost certainly defeat any inexperienced opponent, regardless of size or strength differences.

Ironically, such performance is unlikely to actually be witnessed, since the convictions of such individuals do conduce them into not displaying their skills frivolously. Even when provoked they are known to camouflage their strength to the point of permitting it to be mistaken for weakness, or even cowardice.

Rarely falling from grace, they will allow verbal challenges to bounce off their thick skin and simply walk away from senseless confrontation. If at all possible, they will tactfully defuse most opponents' aggressions through acute wisdom and disarming humbleness. A Master will not strike unless a physical threat is actually made towards him or those that he deems to protect. Even then, his power is always controlled in direct proportion to the level of danger offered by an opponent.

He may try to just demoralize him by blocking any futile strike attempts with lightening-speed. He may even signal the danger of his strength and discourage an attacker by way of directing his otherwise devastating blow into, perhaps, breaking a door or a table next to the opponent.

Such harmony of power and benevolence truly represents the balance found in a Master's self-control, within the spirit of the Martial Arts.

UPHOLDING TRADITION

Considering the fact that martial Arts have expanded so far away from their initial cultural ties, it is actually remarkable that so many of its old traditions have survived to date.

One of the basic aspects of the old structure started with the premise that the Master was a socially established individual, financially independent from his students. In most cases, he was a respected member of a religious or military order whose aspirations were a far cry from those of modern-day Martial Artist-businessmen.

To make it work today under such different values many compromises have been made. So, if you are looking for a setting somewhat similar to the one portrayed in the TV series[3] "Kung-Fu", let me disenchant you right now, for chances are that this would be an unlikely find.

In order to gracefully maintain the traditional discipline and ethical behavior characteristic to the Martial Arts, an instructor's actions must derive from one fundamental intention: the above all intent of cultivating a student's spirit through the improvement of his physical and mental strength.

There are two most common deviations from this principle:

First, when financial gain dictates and justifies an instructor's actions.

---

[3] 1972-1974, 62 episodes.

Many times, individuals will build some elusive pedestals and surround themselves by myth in order to best impress the less knowledgeable into emptying their wallets, and;

Second, and perhaps worst aspect, is when an instructor tries to inflict disciplinary measures, physical or verbal, as means of feeding his own egotistical weakness.

Regardless of its being done intentionally or subconsciously, this all too often can be observed, not only from insecure and less proficient instructors, but even from overly confident ones whose skills and strength carry some weight. They end up creating their own little worlds where they can be absolute rulers for the unfortunate purpose of combatting their own insecurities.

Current twenty-first century eastern culture may have made it impossible for teachers to use physical disciplinary measures in the classrooms, but in the Martial Arts school that can easily be disregarded. Don't get me wrong, what I mean to put in question is the intentions of who may apply such measures, not their actual use or value which I believe can be good if properly used.

These are among the few institutions in this country where one can still use the respect and disciplinary benefits that come from the fear of undergoing physical punishment (even if it is never actually used).

However, under no circumstances should this serve for an instructor to display how tough he may be, not to senselessly push someone around.

One day, while visiting a friend's school, I was invited by him to help with a promotion test. As the event came to its final stage, it caught me totally unprepared as I helplessly watched each member of the judging panel proceed down the line of students, punching them in the abdomen with excessive power and total disregard for age or gender.

This was obviously a customary ritual in that school, for even some of the younger children would take the punches from the instructors and promptly return to their positions, nevertheless plundering their integrity, as it was attested by their suppressed cry and slight convulsion. As discretely as possible I respectfully forfeited my turn to participate in that portion of the test.

Even if the instructor's intentions were to only make his students tougher, this was definitely a case where the end did not justify the means.

Although this does not meet with my training methods, I would have an easier time accepting it if the students were adults testing for a high rank and to whom such imposition would constitute a challenge and a chance to display their strength, rather than a child's dreadful moment of fear.

I enjoyed the couple of months of tough sparring in that school, and I hope that one day my friend will honor me with the reading of this book so he will better understand the reasons for my consequent refraining.

It is not really that hard to form a rule by which an instructor's use of his strength is acceptable, all that's necessary is a little common sense.

*

Junior was my youngest senior ranking student, who had come to us already as a Red Belt. By policy, I always accepted any rank that a student may have attained somewhere else, even if, like in this case, to bring him up to standard nearly two years passed before any further advancement in the color belt system took place.

It was his first summer back from college and now, not only had found new confidence in his taller stature, but also his skills had gained the sharpness that came with the strength of his age.

In preparation for an upcoming competition, we had formed a fighting ring and were taking turns, rotating the positions of fighter and corner judge. Junior, whose nickname had become unfitting of his size, had definitely come a long way, and to everyone's delight, as he pared against me, was putting up a much better fight than what everyone anticipated.

All in good fun, and while encouraging his efforts, the corner judges, composed of my senior ranking students, had started to not award me any points unless Junior himself agreed with the decision. This, inevitably, led to a gradual increase in intensity which he really seemed to enjoy and I, quite frankly, secretly struggled to maintain. Needless to say, by the end, we were hitting considerably hard. So much so that, somehow, it became explicitly determined that the match would only end at the surrender or knockout of one of us.

I honestly expected only to score a good point. But as my spinning back fist made contact with his chin, I heard his forced exhalation and knew immediately he was in trouble. It took almost a minute to bring him back to consciousness and since he appeared lucid, and in no time was making jokes, I didn't insist much when he refused to let me drive him home.

Later that same evening, when checking on his condition by phone, I learned that he had no recollection of driving home not of anything that had happened after the knockout. It had been a bad mistake to let him leave after suffering a concussion.

I never really got to enjoy the glory of my victory nor the rejoicing of my senior students, and I definitely cheated myself from enjoying any of Junior's conceivably newfound respect for my ability, because I was too worried about his well-being.

But anyway, I believe that all the students walked out of that situation in good spirits, and even Junior never really lost face, for I made sure that the talk going around the school emphasized the great fight he put up rather than the way it ended.

To resume my earlier point of view, it was never a question of softness or toughness that moved my actions, but rather a belief that an instructor must always be gradual and well-intended in the use of his strength and must always be careful of how, when, and upon whom he uses it. This can actually become counter-productive for any young instructors still trying to continue their own training simultaneously with managing a school.

Fighting the beginner students is not without its learning value, but if that becomes constant can actually prevent the development of one's own potential. This is one of many other reasons why traditionally it used to be that one was already a fourth degree, in his middle age, to consider opening his own school.

Having had his fill of physical glory and faced with chronological decline, a more patient, more benevolent, more Master-like individual emerges, more naturally apt to find teaching his new way to continue to excel.

Still about tradition, in ancient times students would often pay their Master's teachings through personal offering of food, clothing, or any other services or goods, proper to each one's metier. Such offerings could range anywhere from a good used winter coat to remodeling the roof of the Master's schoolhouse or helping with any maintenance.

Carried over the years this tradition has somehow lost its reciprocation since the business-oriented contemporary establishments, beyond requiring monetary compensation for the teaching services, often will take advantage of this heritage feeling with abusive demands from the students.

The state of mind implemented in this respect should not exceed the one in the case of a school teacher who would kindly accept an apple from his favorite student, and under no circumstances should it be allowed to become manipulated into profit.

As an example, every Friday evening after the last class, I used to clean the mirrors and vacuum the training area, with the occasional voluntary help of some of my students. Since they were paying for my instruction, I always felt that I had no right to demand their help with such tasks. So, if ever I did have their help, it was always offered voluntarily. However, that never stopped me, or the senior students, from once in a while ordering the novices to clean the mirrors that didn't need cleaning, or vacuum the floor, that didn't need vacuuming, as a disciplinary act, or as a part of the process to develop a spirit of humbleness.

If because of one's profession (whether he is a doctor or a plumber) a student would volunteer to somehow contribute with his expertise to the welfare of the school, I would always credit their account proportionately.

I remember the complaints from several colleagues of mine, students at a Taekwondo school, where the so-called "Master" would abusively expect to be rendered their services as accountants, merchants, etc., absolutely free and this despite his unforgiving demand for some rather exorbitant teaching fee.

Another aspect of abusive demands that I always found unreasonable is how so many instructors unscrupulously obligate the more advanced students to teach classes for beginners. At times students may be called upon to, sporadically and within reason, assist the instructor by teaching some portions of the class while he may be temporarily detained.

There really is a fine line in determining where the abuse starts, especially since in most cases the brainwash actually makes the student proudly accept the teaching duty as a given honor. Sometimes reality does not hit until the student finds himself regimented into a schedule of teaching and having to arrange his life around it to avoid falling from grace at the "Master's" eyes.

Although the act of teaching can contribute in certain aspects to the development of a Martial Artist, it really is a considerably small benefit if compared to the free vital help it provides the school owner. After all, what could be better than having all the classes taught by people who are willing and honored to work for free.

I could not possibly let this opportunity pass by without mentioning an old friend who, at one time, found himself cornered in just such a situation. After many years of dedication, one day he was finally faced with the reality of the situation and decided to break his ties with the abusive teacher and open his own school.

Even though his supervision of all the different levels of teaching is almost constant, all the assistant instructors are <u>volunteer</u>, qualified Black Belt students, whose services have been exchanged for a free membership in his school. This is an exception to the rule, a rare and honest arrangement that many instructors could learn from. (Might I add, that this is not a bad addition to all the other good reasons why Black Belt students might want to stay longer.)

Unlike during previous eras, these days, to learn Martial Arts it is unlikely that one would have to first gain a Master's graces by enduring the most demeaning tasks of the school, such as: spending months brushing wood floors with soap and water and doing the laundry and cooking for the senior students. The setting has changed considerably, but even if modernized, that is still no reason to lose old principles of spirit and discipline.

Although instruction starts right away, new students must still endure the lengthy and less exciting basics of training. During the first few months, they should never even get to spar and will not really get to learn effective techniques nor develop any potentially dangerous power. With all its other reasons to be, this due process also acts as filtration for some of the bad apples.

Even though Martial Arts can often have a positive influence on most students and even play a correctional role, at times, fundamental aspects of character formed by previous education (or lack of it) can become almost impossible to correct.

The danger of teaching the wrong individual is always present and should be part of an instructor's concerns and abilities to evaluate all students' psychological aptness (even if only superficially).

Of course, it must go without saying that the financial concerns of a school owner should never prevent him from refusing a student who may somehow have been deemed unfit to learn Fighting Art.

An increasingly growing number of individuals that give Martial Artists a bad reputation is the fruit of just such absence of selection. This forms a particularly bad alliance with the irresponsible violence displayed in today's movies, where actors are taught to mimic some of the most brutal and advanced techniques, that were never meant to be taught without first educating someone in preparation for such knowledge.

Teaching a fighting Art without traditional spirit can ultimately lead to such disastrous results as the extreme of offering someone a loaded gun without first providing the knowledge necessary to make its use of responsible, wise, and honorable.

Depending on how open-minded a student can be the process of instilling these qualities is usually a lengthy endeavor – one rarely endured by many. The vast majority of all individuals who start Marshal Art never achieve the Black Belt rank. In fact, most people normally drop out during the first three months.

The most common reason for this is the realization that it is not as easy as learning a few secret tricks that will overnight turn them into invincible fighters with supernatural powers. It takes years of patient methodic training to become proficient.

In the beginning, I also quested for such powers. I shall never forget my disappointment when I was finally awarded by Black Belt. That day my own experience confirmed the words of one of my instructors, whom I had refused to believe for a long time, when he repeatedly told me that in Karate there were no secrets, only hard work.

I remember feeling more confident about being able to defend myself against an assailant during the time I was a Blue Belt than that day when my expectations of becoming "Superman" did not come true. Long after that day, I came to realize that such a state of mind was just the result of my approaching the same level of understanding as then reached by that instructor. I later found that there are, in fact, many secrets in Karate. The difficulty is that they are based on certain feelings that can only be developed through years of personal experience.

Different instructors, when referring to the persistence and patience synonymous with Martial Arts training will often quote cliches such as:

"Like soft water on hard rock."

Understanding the meaning of such euphemisms may be relatively easy, but to actually assimilate and convert it into practice is one of the many aspects separating the Master from disciple.

I remember one day while visiting the cathedral in the Vatican City in Italy getting separated from my group as they continued following the tour guide and I had remained admiring a statue of one of the Patron Saints.

Scaled at least twice the size of a man, it displayed a perfectly detailed left foot, wearing a sandal, however where the right foot should have been there remained only a perfectly polished thin plaque of metal. As the guide had explained, such erosion was incredibly caused by billions of people throughout the years passing by and traditionally touching that part with their hands.

All of a sudden, I found myself so submerged in my thoughts that I lost complete track of time. Already picturing myself using this story to illustrate my explanations to my students, I don't know exactly how long I may have stood there as people passing by in silent respect would take me for another faithful follower, absorbed in reverent prayer.

The development of a Martial Artist's spirit is not a casual circumstance that arises coincidentally. It is rather a methodical process, often guided by very specific guidelines. These guidelines are normally presented in the form of an honor code, which most schools will usually display on one of their walls.

As dictated by the tradition of their particular style they may even, at times, initiate and/or finish training sessions by making the students recite it out loud.

Such a list should be comprised of updated and sensible tenants which the students can identify with and to whom these are applicable. I still remember a code taught in one of the schools that I attended as a beginner:

- Be loyal to your nation

- Be obedient to your parents
- Be loving to your spouse
- Be honorable to your friends
- Make a just kill.

The first tenant was for me the most controversial; obviously, a principle carried from the militaristic structure of previous times. In those days when the most sophisticated weaponry was limited to the sword or the bow and arrow, hand-to-hand combat played a major role in the result of a battle. For that reason, the knowledge of Martial Art was a threat that advocated no less prejudice than today's nuclear bomb secrets.

Besides the fact that Martial Arts have long been surpassed by modern warfare, losing military value, personally, I have additional reasons to feel uncomfortable with the first quote, within this context:

A political revolution that radically changed my native country had given me such an eye-opening political education that I made the vow to never again have anything to do with politics and to keep myself as distant as possible from any government.

I must clarify that my position is not to uphold anarchy. I very much believe in law and order, it is the usual abuses of authority, the lack of honor, and the corruption that force my distance.

If there are any patriots that contend that not all governments may deserve such predisposition, I cannot help wondering what kind of history books they can possibly be reading, that still allow them to be that naïve.

By obeying the first dogma – "Be loyal to your nation" – one may be forced to, literally, break the last – "Make a just kill" if one lived in a Nazi society, again, obeying such a command would undoubtedly

Master or Myth

force him to break all the other previously listed codes of honor. But, anyway, that, by itself, could be the subject of another book.

Following the list of tenants, being "obedient to my parents" was good advice, but back then, as an independent young adult, it seemed a little patronizing and uncalled for.

"Be loving to my spouse:" My wife today says that this one worked on me...but back then, being single (like the majority of my fellow students) had little or no inspirational value.

So, in the end, I was left with the belief that only the last two tenets were worth something to me.

"Being honorable to friends" made perfectly good sense, even if it seemed it should not be limited to only friends.

"Making a just kill", although it may have been better expressed by simply saying: "Always be fair." I ended up accepting it since there was a certain impact in that wording that always made people pay better attention.

Many years later, in my own school, a Code was displayed reading:

- "Be loving to your family
- Be honorable in your actions
- Be humble at your strongest
- Make a just kill."

The addition of humbleness is, I believe, a fundamental one.

Humbleness will instill appropriate behavior, calm thought, controlled and intelligent expression, and execution of one's intentions. It ultimately leads to respect from others. A great imbalance can arise from the unconformity of those who, having conquered strength along the way, failed to also find humbleness.

*

I was sixteen years of age and, together with my friends, as usual, I was riding the train from our hometown to go to school. Like myself, most of them belonged to the local Sports Center Club, where we took Judo and shared an insatiable curiosity about anything having to do with Martial Arts.

That day we had particularly noticed the two men seated across from us, because one of them was carrying a Martial Art uniform, neatly rolled and tied together by a brown color belt. Granted that he was a robust looking individual, but to us kids, the mere sight of the brown belt made him look ten times stronger.

Undeniably noticing our admiration, he had repositioned himself on the seat, intentionally flexing his muscular arms and inflating his chest like a rooster about to claim its territory.

My dwindling admiration was already changing to saturation, but by the time he started cracking his knuckles, I was already thinking that after all he really didn't look so strong – in fact he was actually kind of short, I thought.

Trying to ignore his presence my eyes wondered, seeking something more interesting to see, when I accidently noticed the man seated next to him. Since they had been speaking to each other once in a while I was obviously thinking that they were traveling together.

If he was as athletic as the "rooster man" it was impossible to tell because his clothing was not as revealing, but given the intellectual looking glasses through which his undivided attention focused on his little book, he didn't exactly appear to be the warrior type. It was as if he was trying to hide the subject of his book, having its cover so neatly bonded in plain brown paper.

Master or Myth

The train was already approaching the next station, so he closed his book and placed it inside his gym bag that was on the floor held between his feet. He inadvertently exposed his own uniform which was tied by an old worn-out black belt. So surprised I was, with my jaw hanging open by then, it would have been impossible for him not to notice my intrusion into my secrecy.

The two flaps of his bag were suddenly brought together by his hands, as these would clap together abruptly closing it and startling me looking up again. As our eyes met, he simply and nonchalantly gave me a quick wink and without ever changing the stone-cold expression on his face, he swiftly disappeared among the other passengers that were also leaving the train.

As I had walked up to the window trying to get a last glimpse of the mystery man, a few seconds had passed before my trance was broken by an arm evolving around my neck, as my friend started fooling around and said:

"With him, you wouldn't want to mess…right!"

At first, I didn't quite understand his comment, but realizing that he was, in fact, referring to the arrogant "rooster man", I quickly freed myself of his choke-hold, making my elbow strike his exposed ribs with the usual lacking kindness of child's play. As my other friends chuckled, and he complained about my blow, I impetuously replied:

I would take him on, with one hand tied behind my back…It's the other guy that I wouldn't want to mess with!"

I was about to justify my reply when another one of our friends entering the train in that same station, asking euphorically if we had noticed the Karate National Champion, who had just left the train. He was, of course, referring to the man with the mystery book who, incidentally, did become my first Karate instructor, and always used to advise his students to bind any Martial Art book in plain brown paper before reading it in public.

It really is amazing how the apparent insignificant event that took place that day in the train could actually have such a great influence on my young, impressionable, mind. Since that day, never again did I carry my Judo uniform publicly without properly concealing it.

Whether I knew it right then or not, that was to become one of my first lesson in humility. A lesson I would never forget and would always treasure with respect and admiration.

As confidence grows, the fact that humbleness tends to diminish makes it a difficult quality to maintain, and even harder to attain if, like most people, by nature one did not already have it in the beginning. However, and for that reason, the ironic presence of humbleness in the high levels of Martial Arts makes it that much more difficult of a quality to find and most certainly a more venerable one to possess.

*

As the most important tournament of the season approached, training had become progressively more intense over the course of the last two months. That night the students prepared for one of the many usual drills. This one consisted of one student trying to strike the handheld shield before the other could move it out of range. The objective was to sharpen the offensive and defensive reflexes of the respective participants.

As on numerous previous occasions, Sato, whose shield was being handled by the Master, already anticipated the usual frustration of not being able to even touch it before it was expertly moved out of his range. For this reason, when for the first time his punch managed to slightly graze the shield, a newfound confidence seemed to magically increase his speed.

That night, even the senior instructors praised Sato for actually being able to, sporadically, land three or four full-force blows before the Master could withdraw the shield.

Overwhelmed in satisfaction, Sato, whose personality had not yet matured in the ways of the Martial Arts, couldn't contain his boisterous excitement. Rather than graciously bow to all the compliments, or perhaps encourage his peers into believing that their own ability could not be far from making them capable of doing the same, he arrogantly scorned those who failed to match his deed.

A few weeks had passed and Sato's superb performance at the tournament had already been left behind, lost in the struggle of the new challenges at hand. Sato could hardly believe how that day the Master would move the handheld shield so fast that it made all his attempts appear slower than ever before.

As frustration started to impede his performance, the old Master stopped and said:

You must understand that before the competition when practicing this drill, we meant to improve your confidence and speed, but today we seek to gain upon your humbleness."

Sato was not quite sure of what made him feel worse; discovering that what had allowed him to strike the shield before was his Master's intention rather than his own presumed improvement in speed, or how, at the time, with all his pomposity, he had really made a fool of himself.

Unaware that the invocating of such feelings was just another step towards his education in the spirit of the Martial Arts, and from his immediate perspective he could only dread the anticipated teasing that was sure to come from the senior students.

So, his lesson would continue when back in the dressing rooms, one of the senior students sympathetically slapped his shoulder saying:

"Don't worry, we have all been through it before. It's just a phase of your training and, in time, you will also learn."

THE SPROUTING SEED

Like any successful planting demands a proper season, methodic care, and nourishment, so does the novice requires all aspects of proper instruction.

These days Martial Arts training tends to emphasize aspects of self-defense, physical conditioning, and discipline. The first two attracts the kids, and the last normally draws the parents into accepting the sacrifice of paying the not so inexpensive fees, sometimes as an effort to provide their children the discipline missing from their normal education.

However, rarely can one find a sincere and knowledgeable dedication to the fact that it can also lead to spiritual development, perhaps the most important benefit of all.

The repetitive practice of self-defense allows the students to eventually learn the actual mechanics of a variety of techniques. Through conditioning, the hands and feet will be transformed into effective weapons and, through sparring, the reflexes and awareness will become sharper.

According to the actual quality of instruction and genetically related potential, a compatible level of efficiency will eventually be attained. The usual physical enhancements of calisthenics and stretching exercises will become obvious. Basic techniques, forms, sit-ups, push-ups, and back and leg stretches will all contribute to toning the muscles and improving endurance in order to better prepare the body for the training ahead.

Dexterity, balance, and coordination being the mirrors of one's mental control, will be developed in harmony with proper breathing, guided by the help of "Kiai". The spirit will be fortified by way of allowing the novice a high rate of success and the building of self-confidence. As it grows, so will the obstacles methodically become harder to overcome in an endless process designed for continuous stimulation of all the various aspects of personal growth.

Just as the higher endurance will allow the body new ranges of physical activity, so will better concentration and visualization develop a stronger mind, enabling it to push the already above normal limitations even further, making it at times <u>appear</u> supernatural.

A mentally disciplined student of less physical ability will eventually prevail over a less mentally disciplined student with higher physical ability.

So, remember:

If while sparring you fumble, you are lacking physical control;

If your mind wanders out of focus between the commands of an instructor, you are lacking mental control;

If your humbleness fades when tested, you are lacking spiritual control.

The absence of one or more of these qualities will make you less than a Martial Artist.

On the other hand, the proportionate composite of the above-mentioned qualities will lead to levels of powerful understanding and well-being. A state of body, mind, and spirit that is only attainable through enduring personal experience and cannot be replaced by any theoretical teachings.

THE MENTAL NUTRIENT

I guess it would be fair to say that Martial Arts, despite all its constant challenges, became part of my daily life with relative ease. From my youth, my parents provided me with an education that incorporated many aspects similar to those preached by Martial Arts codes.

My father is a living example of an indomitable spirit, and always taught me to be fair and honest and to not give ground when fighting for my convictions. My mother, in her unmatched kindness, played a balancing role in instilling all qualities of a more compassionate nature.

On a physical aspect, the hardships of training were really just replacing the very young years when I had practiced gymnastics. During that time while trying to learn very difficult and dangerous skills, I had already learned to endure and "enjoy" the pains of rigorous training.

So, in all honesty, what attracted me to Martial Arts was the possibility of learning to better defend myself and for a long time, it was the thrill of fighting that made me stay. But, of course, at that time I was only seeing the tip of the iceberg.

Martial Arts can be many different things to many different people. I believe that over the years it has given me considerable ability to defend myself (as I had hoped), and it has certainly been full of challenges.

Becoming used to controlling emotions and enduring the pains of fighting is a great preparation to face any possible hardships that life may present. I always believed that beyond the obvious, this was one of the most noble purposes for fighting in the Martial Arts.

As a child being raised in a strongly social class-conscious country, I was already enchanted with the Martial Arts of the noble European knights, but when I was first exposed to the oriental version, the Samurai, surrounded by all its mysteries, it added an irresistible appeal to my romantic ideals. Unexpectedly, however, it eventually led me to a new personal philosophy. One which, in fact, became applicable to all other situations of daily life.

This realization derived from my endless search for the end of the road and was inspired by the words of an old Master, who defied true mastery as one's ability to maintain inner peace in all situations.

As simplistic as it may appear, this would be the ultimate mental nutrient:

The total embodying of the Martial Arts spirit, where, in enlightened wisdom, one would learn to make no mistakes in all his actions, and therefore to be able to remain pleased with oneself, which – after all – is the ultimate test and goal.

www.ingramcontent.com/pod-product-compliance
Lightning Source LLC
Chambersburg PA
CBHW072012030526
44119CB00064B/672